U.S. ENVIRONMENTAL PROTECTION AGENCY

OFFICE OF INSPECTOR GENERAL

EPA Inaction in Identifying Hazardous Waste Pharmaceuticals May Result in Unsafe Disposal

Report No. 12-P-0508   May 25, 2012

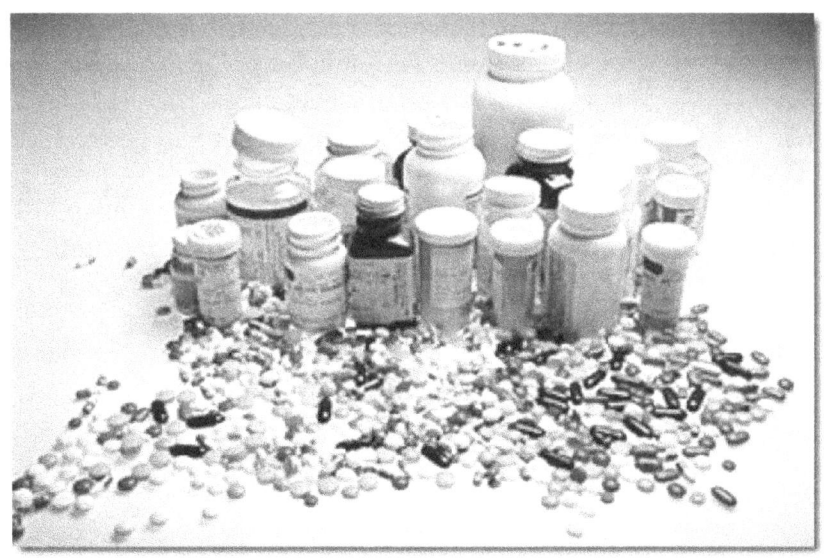

Report Contributors: Carolyn Copper
                              Steve Hanna
                              Roopa Batni
                              Tapati Bhattacharyya
                              Brooke Shull

Abbreviations

BMP	Best Management Practice
EPA	U.S. Environmental Protection Agency
GAO	U.S. Government Accountability Office
HWPs	Hazardous waste pharmaceuticals
NIOSH	National Institute for Occupational Safety and Health
OIG	Office of Inspector General
ORCR	Office of Resource Conservation and Recovery
OSHA	Occupational Safety and Health Administration
OSWER	Office of Solid Waste and Emergency Response
RCRA	Resource Conservation and Recovery Act
UWR	Universal Waste Rule

Cover photo: Examples of pharmaceuticals. (EPA photo)

Hotline

To report fraud, waste, or abuse, contact us through one of the following methods:

e-mail:	OIG_Hotline@epa.gov	**write:**	EPA Inspector General Hotline
phone:	1-888-546-8740		1200 Pennsylvania Avenue NW
fax:	202-566-2599		Mailcode 2431T
online:	http://www.epa.gov/oig/hotline.htm		Washington, DC 20460

At a Glance

Why We Did This Review

We conducted this review to evaluate the U.S. Environmental Protection Agency's (EPA's) process to identify and appropriately classify pharmaceuticals as hazardous waste and to ensure their safe disposal.

Background

The discovery of a variety of pharmaceuticals in water has raised concerns about potentially adverse environmental consequences of these contaminants. Studies have suggested the detection of pharmaceutical compounds in treated wastewater effluent, streams, lakes, seawater, drinking water, and groundwater, as well as in sediments and fish tissue. EPA has the authority under the Resource Conservation and Recovery Act (RCRA) to regulate hazardous waste pharmaceuticals (HWPs) to ensure safe management and disposal practices.

For further information, contact our Office of Congressional and Public Affairs at (202) 566-2391.

The full report is at:
www.epa.gov/oig/reports/2012/
20120525-12-P-0508.pdf

EPA Inaction in Identifying Hazardous Waste Pharmaceuticals May Result in Unsafe Disposal

What We Found

Since 1980, EPA has not used its RCRA authority to determine whether pharmaceuticals may qualify as hazardous waste. EPA also has not established a process for the regular identification and review of pharmaceuticals that may qualify for regulation as hazardous waste. Without a regular process, EPA cannot provide assurance that pharmaceuticals that may pose a hazardous risk to human health and the environment have been identified. We identified eight chemicals found in pharmaceuticals that meet EPA's criteria for regulation as acute hazardous waste, but wastes containing these chemicals are not regulated as such. There are over 100 drugs that federal occupational safety organizations have identified as hazardous but may not have been reviewed by EPA to determine whether they may qualify as hazardous waste. EPA staff stated they have started examining these drugs for listing as hazardous waste. Further, the state of Minnesota recently noted that there has been a proliferation of pharmaceutical development since RCRA regulations were established. Our review has identified a risk that there are unknown but potentially dangerous unregulated HWPs that may be unsafely disposed and released into the environment.

An additional challenge to ensuring the safe disposal of HWPs is that some health care facilities, such as hospitals, may be unaware of federal hazardous waste regulations. The state of Minnesota, for example, has reported that there is a "general lack of awareness by the health care industry of RCRA regulatory requirements." This may result in mismanagement of hazardous waste pharmaceuticals.

In 2008, EPA proposed an amendment to the Universal Waste Rule to address pharmaceutical wastes. However, no action on the Rule has occurred since the close of the public comments period in 2009. During our review, EPA staff informed us that the Agency has decided to develop another proposal for the regulation of hazardous waste pharmaceuticals at health care facilities. EPA staff stated that "due to substantial negative public comments received on the 2008 universal waste proposal, the Agency is developing a revised proposal for regulation of hazardous waste pharmaceuticals at healthcare facilities." EPA anticipates the proposal will be available for public comment in spring 2013.

What We Recommend

We recommend that EPA establish a process to review pharmaceuticals for regulation as hazardous waste and develop an outreach and compliance assistance plan for health care facilities managing HWPs.

UNITED STATES ENVIRONMENTAL PROTECTION AGENCY
WASHINGTON, D.C. 20460

May 25, 2012

MEMORANDUM

SUBJECT: EPA Inaction in Identifying Hazardous Waste Pharmaceuticals May Result in Unsafe Disposal
Report No. 12-P-0508

FROM: Arthur A. Elkins, Jr.

TO: Mathy Stanislaus
Assistant Administrator for Solid Waste and Emergency Response

This is our report on the subject evaluation conducted by the Office of Inspector General (OIG) of the U.S. Environmental Protection Agency (EPA). This report contains findings that describe the problems the OIG has identified and corrective actions the OIG recommends. This report represents the opinion of the OIG and does not necessarily represent the final EPA position. Final determinations on matters in this report will be made by EPA managers in accordance with established resolution procedures.

Action Required

In accordance with EPA Manual 2750, you are required to provide a written response to this report within 90 calendar days. The recommendations are listed as unresolved because planned completion dates were not provided. Your response should include a corrective action plan for agreed-upon actions, including actual or estimated milestone completion dates. Your response will be posted on the OIG's public website, along with our comments on your response. Your response should be provided in an Adobe PDF file that complies with the accessibility requirements of Section 508 of the Rehabilitation Act of 1973, as amended. Please e-mail your response to Carolyn Copper at copper.carolyn@epa.gov. If your response contains data that you do not want to be released to the public, you should identify the data for redaction. We have no objections to the further release of this report to the public.

If you or your staff have any questions regarding this report, please contact Carolyn Copper at (202) 566-0829 or copper.carolyn@epa.gov, or Steve Hanna at (415) 947-4527 or hanna.steve@epa.gov.

Table of Contents

Chapters

Appendices

Chapter 1
Introduction

Purpose

The purpose of this review was to evaluate the U.S. Environmental Protection Agency's (EPA's) process to identify and appropriately classify pharmaceuticals as hazardous waste and to ensure their safe disposal. We addressed the following questions:

1. Do EPA's hazardous waste codes appropriately classify pharmaceuticals as hazardous waste?
2. What process has EPA established to identify and list new pharmaceuticals as hazardous waste?
3. What steps have states taken to identify and regulate additional pharmaceuticals as hazardous waste?
4. How will the Universal Waste Rule (UWR) impact the management of hazardous waste pharmaceuticals (HWPs)? What is the current status of the rule?

Background

The discovery of a variety of pharmaceuticals in surface, ground, and drinking waters around the country has raised concerns about the potentially adverse environmental consequences of these contaminants. Although the effects on humans are unknown, the U.S. Government Accountability Office (GAO) reports that some research has demonstrated the potential impact to human health from exposure to pharmaceuticals found in drinking water, such as antibiotics and those that interfere with human hormone development. In addition, minute concentrations of some pharmaceuticals can have detrimental effects on aquatic species, such as hormonal imbalances leading to feminization and reproductive problems in fish populations. Studies have suggested the detection of pharmaceutical compounds in treated wastewater effluent, streams, lakes, seawater, and groundwater, as well as in sediments and fish tissue. For example, during 1999 and 2000, the United States Geological Survey conducted a study of 139 streams across the country and detected pharmaceutical compounds in 80 percent of the streams sampled.

In the 2008 proposed universal waste rule, EPA defines a pharmaceutical as any chemical product, vaccine, or allergenic, not containing a radioactive component, that is intended for use in the diagnosis, cure, mitigation, treatment, or prevention of disease or injury in humans or animals. This definition also refers to any product with the primary purpose of dispensing or delivering a pharmaceutical.

Pharmaceutical waste[1] includes expired drugs, personal medications, waste materials containing excess drugs (syringes, IV bags, tubing, vials, etc.), and drugs that are intended to be discarded. Generators of hazardous waste pharmaceuticals (HWPs) include: pharmacies, physicians' and dentists' offices, outpatient care centers, ambulatory health care services, residential care facilities, veterinary clinics, and reverse distributors.[2] Health care facilities may dispose of unused pharmaceuticals, especially residues, down the drain (e.g., intravenous (IV) bags emptied into the sink). According to EPA, for many years, a standard disposal practice at many health care facilities was to flush unused pharmaceuticals down the toilet or drain. Although the domestic sewage exclusion generally allows facilities to flush pharmaceuticals down the drain, EPA believes that facilities should not dispose of their pharmaceuticals down the drain.

EPA Definition of Hazardous Waste

Under the Resource Conservation and Recovery Act (RCRA), EPA has the authority to regulate the generation, storage, transportation, treatment, and disposal of hazardous waste. Most states have been delegated the primary responsibility for regulating RCRA hazardous waste. Any facility, such as hospitals and other health facilities that generate more than 100 kg (220 lbs.) of hazardous waste per month, or greater than 1 kg (2.2 lbs.) of acute hazardous waste per month, are subject to RCRA hazardous waste regulations. RCRA requires that hazardous wastes be transported in approved containers to permitted hazardous waste disposal facilities by a hazardous waste transporter. RCRA prohibits disposal of hazardous waste in municipal waste landfills, municipal incinerators, or medical waste plants.[3]

EPA's RCRA regulations establish two ways of identifying hazardous waste:

1. Characteristic hazardous waste – A waste may be considered hazardous if it exhibits one of the four defined characteristics of hazardous waste:

    a. Ignitability – wastes that can readily catch fire and maintain combustion.
    b. Corrosivity – wastes that are acidic or alkaline (basic).
    c. Reactivity – wastes that readily explode or undergo violent reactions or react by releasing toxic gases or fumes.
    d. Toxicity – wastes likely to leach dangerous concentrations of toxic chemicals into groundwater.

---

[1] Under RCRA, EPA does not regulate pharmaceuticals until they are discarded as waste.
[2] Reverse distributors are private companies that provide a service to the health care industry by keeping track of manufacturer unused pharmaceutical reimbursement policies, and thus get health care facilities credit for the pharmaceuticals prior to sending them off-site for disposal.
[3] RCRA excludes hazardous waste generated by households from the definition of hazardous waste.

2. Listed hazardous waste – EPA may also explicitly identify hazardous wastes through a listing process. Lists of hazardous waste developed by EPA are:

    a. F-list (wastes from non-specific sources) – hazardous wastes from certain common industrial and manufacturing processes.
    b. K-list (wastes from specific industries).
    c. P- and U- lists of chemicals – hazardous wastes including specific unused chemicals. Chemicals are included on the U-list based on toxicity or other characteristics. Chemicals are included on the P-list if they are acutely toxic. P-list chemicals are regulated when generated in lower quantities than U-list chemicals.

P-listed wastes are identified as acute hazardous waste because the waste has been found to be fatal to humans or animals above certain thresholds/doses. EPA can regulate a waste as acutely hazardous if it has been shown in studies to have:

- an oral Lethal Dose 50[4] toxicity for rats of less than 50 milligrams per kilogram,
- an inhalation Lethal Concentration 50 toxicity for rats of less than 2 milligrams per liter, or
- a dermal Lethal Dose 50 toxicity for rabbits of less than 200 milligrams per kilogram

EPA also can regulate a waste as acutely hazardous if it is capable of causing or significantly contributing to an increase in serious irreversible or incapacitating reversible illness.

Pharmaceuticals can be included on the U-list if they exhibit any of the four hazardous characteristics described above, or if they contain a toxic constituent and are capable of posing a "substantial present or potential hazard to human health or the environment when improperly treated, stored, transported, or disposed of, or otherwise managed." Toxic constituents identified by RCRA are chemical compounds or elements which scientific studies show to have toxic, carcinogenic (i.e., cancer-causing), mutagenic (i.e., causing genetic mutation which can lead to cancer), or teratogenic (i.e., causing birth defects) effects on humans or other life forms.

Volume of Hazardous Waste Pharmaceuticals

According to EPA, pharmaceuticals are commonly used for diagnosing, treating, or preventing an extremely broad range of medical problems and for cosmetic and lifestyle purposes. HWPs are generated by a large number of facilities from different sectors across the country. However, estimates of the volume of HWPs

---

[4] The LD50 and LC50 value is a measure of acute toxicity, and indicates the ability of a toxic or poisonous substance to kill half the population in animal studies after a specified test duration.

may be understated because of EPA's failure to identify any new HWPs since 1980. In addition, volumes may be understated because EPA believes that many health care facilities, such as hospitals, are unaware of their RCRA reporting obligations[5] for hazardous waste. Further, federal regulations require only large quantity generators to report their hazardous waste generation types and volumes to EPA. EPA estimates that hospitals and reverse distributors generate about 15,000 tons of HWPs each year. We note that, by itself, volume is not the only meaningful measure of the potential HWP problem, as many pharmaceuticals are toxic at very low concentrations.

EPA's Best Management Practices Guidance for Pharmaceuticals

EPA has taken some action to address concerns about possible effects on human health and the environment from the release of pharmaceuticals into the environment. In August 2010, EPA's Office of Water issued a draft guidance document, *Best Management Practices for Unused Pharmaceuticals at Health Care Facilities*. As defined in this guidance, EPA's goal is to keep pharmaceuticals out of U.S. waters. The guidance recommends best management practices (BMPs) to be used by health care facilities (e.g., hospitals) to minimize the release of pharmaceuticals to the environment. EPA identified these BMPs after:

- site visits at 12 health care facilities;
- consulting with over 700 stakeholders, including health care professionals, government entities, health care industry associations, and companies that manage unused pharmaceuticals;
- review of disposal data from 20 hospitals and long-term care facilities (e.g., nursing homes, assisted living facilities); and
- review of literature data, reports, and state recommendations.

The guidance describes BMPs that EPA recommends to health care facilities, long-term care facilities, medical clinics, and doctors' offices, when managing and disposing of unused pharmaceuticals.

EPA's 2008 Universal Waste Rule Amendment to Address Hazardous Waste Pharmaceuticals

In December 2008, EPA proposed to add HWPs to the UWR[6]. The UWR, originally issued on May 11, 1995, modified RCRA hazardous waste regulations by establishing a set of streamlined requirements for the collection of certain widely dispersed hazardous wastes, called "universal wastes." According to

---

[5] Hazardous waste generators producing more than 2,200 pounds of hazardous waste, or more than 2.2 pounds of acute hazardous waste, in a calendar month must report the waste type and volume to EPA every 2 years. The total volume of hazardous waste reported in 2009 was approximately 35 million tons.
[6] Federal Register: December 2, 2008 (Volume 73, Number 232), Page 73519-73544, at http://www.epa.gov/fedrgstr/EPA-WASTE/2008/December/Day-02/f28161.htm.

EPA, the proposed 2008 rule would facilitate better and environmentally sound management of pharmaceutical wastes by streamlining the generator requirements and encouraging generators of HWPs to manage them under the provisions of the UWR. EPA believed this would ensure that HWPs are properly disposed of and treated as hazardous wastes. In 2009, EPA summarized comments on the proposed rule. According to EPA, there was substantial negative comment on the proposed rule such that the Agency decided that it could not address the comments without re-proposing a new rule. EPA has recently stated that the Agency has decided to develop another proposal for health care facility-specific regulations for the management of hazardous waste pharmaceuticals.

Other Federal Agency Hazardous Drug Lists

The National Institute for Occupational Safety and Health (NIOSH) is the federal agency responsible for conducting research and making recommendations for the prevention of work-related injury and illness. NIOSH publishes a List of Antineoplastic (e.g., chemotherapy) and Other Hazardous Drugs in Health Care Settings, also referred to as the NIOSH Drug Alert list, listing what it believes should be handled as hazardous materials. The Occupational Safety and Health Administration (OSHA) hazard communication standard requires facilities to identify hazardous drugs that must be handled using special precautions. OSHA developed a hazardous drug list in the early 1990s and it remains a primary reference for identifying drugs that should be handled as hazardous waste. OSHA lists 61 pharmaceuticals on its hazardous drug list and the latest version of the NIOSH list published in 2010 includes 157 drugs.

Scope and Methodology

We conducted our work from August 2011 to February 2012 in accordance with generally accepted government auditing standards. Those standards require that we plan and perform the evaluation to obtain sufficient, appropriate evidence to provide a reasonable basis for our findings and conclusions based on our objectives. We assessed whether EPA has a systematic process to identify and appropriately classify pharmaceuticals as hazardous waste and to ensure their safe disposal. We believe the evidence obtained provides a reasonable basis for our findings and conclusions based upon our objectives.

We interviewed program and information technology staff of the EPA Office of Resource Conservation and Recovery (ORCR), scientists and program staff of the EPA Office of Research and Development, and staff of the EPA Region 9 Waste Management Division Enforcement. We interviewed state environmental protection program staff from Minnesota, Washington, and California. In addition, we interviewed staff from the U.S. Drug Enforcement Agency's Office of Diversion Control in Washington, DC; and the Director of PharmEcology, a Waste Management company.

We reviewed EPA and state programs, regulations, and guidance documents related to HWPs, including EPA's Proposed UWR and BMP guidance. We also reviewed the following documents to identify potential HWPs and toxicity data:

- EPA P- and U-lists of hazardous waste.
- EPA Endocrine Disruptors list.
- NIOSH Drug Alert list of hazardous pharmaceuticals.
- OSHA Chemical list and Carcinogen list.

Prior Evaluation Coverage

The following Office of Inspector General (OIG) and GAO reports addressed issues related to the scope of our review:

- OIG Report No. 11-P-0215, *EPA's Endocrine Disruptor Screening Program Should Establish Management Controls to Ensure More Timely Results*, May 3, 2011.
- GAO Report No. GAO-11-346, *Environmental Health: Action Needed to Sustain Agencies' Collaboration on Pharmaceuticals in Drinking Water*, August 8, 2011.

Chapter 2
EPA Has Not Used Its Authority to Assess and Manage Potential Hazards of Pharmaceutical Waste

Although EPA has the authority under RCRA, it has not added to its regulations pharmaceuticals that may qualify as hazardous waste since 1980. EPA also has not established a process for the regular identification and review of pharmaceuticals that may qualify for regulation. EPA believes many health care facilities flush HWPs down drains, a potentially harmful disposal method. In 2008, EPA proposed an amendment to the UWR, in part to address health care facilities' unfamiliarity or confusion with RCRA requirements. However, the rule has been stalled since 2009 and EPA just recently decided it would develop another proposal for healthcare facility-specific regulations for the management of HWPs. Given the proliferation of pharmaceutical development since RCRA was enacted, EPA inaction on adding to its regulations pharmaceuticals that qualify as hazardous waste may result in unsafe disposal and releases of dangerous pharmaceuticals into the environment.

EPA Has Not Used Its Hazardous Waste Management Authority

In 1980, EPA identified approximately 31 chemicals used as pharmaceuticals that met the RCRA hazardous waste criteria but EPA has not updated its list since that time. Moreover, EPA has not established a process for the regular identification and review of pharmaceuticals that may qualify for regulation as HWPs. The Food and Drug Administration has approved an average of 30 new drugs each year since 1996. Consequently, RCRA hazardous waste regulations are not keeping up with drug development and the potential hazards they may pose if mismanaged and disposed without the necessary protections to human health and the environment. Without an established process to review pharmaceuticals, EPA cannot ensure that it has identified pharmaceutical contaminants that may pose a hazardous risk to human health and the environment.

Many More Drugs Than EPA Has Identified May Be Hazardous

There are more than 100 drugs that NIOSH and OSHA have identified as hazardous but may not have been reviewed by EPA to determine if they qualify for hazardous waste regulation. We reviewed both lists and identified eight chemicals from the NIOSH list of hazardous pharmaceuticals that meet EPA criteria for regulation as acute hazardous waste, but are not regulated.[7] We also identified three U-list pharmaceuticals that meet P-list criteria based on rat oral LD50 values.[7] Further, we identified at least 21 additional pharmaceuticals with

---

[7] See appendix A for additional details.

LD50 values between 50 and 500 mg/kg, which are within the range of values found for existing U-list pharmaceuticals.[8]

According to EPA's 2010 draft guidance, *Best Management Practices for Unused Pharmaceuticals at Health Care Facilities*, many health care facilities, such as hospitals, use the NIOSH list of hazardous materials to identify unused pharmaceuticals that should be handled similarly to hazardous waste as defined under RCRA. The draft guidance further states that, although RCRA does not require facilities to manage NIOSH-listed hazardous materials the same as RCRA hazardous waste, EPA recommends RCRA guidelines as a BMP for managing NIOSH-listed hazardous materials. Drugs considered hazardous by the NIOSH definition include those that exhibit characteristics in humans or animals, such as carcinogenicity (cancer-causing), reproductive toxicity, organ toxicity at low doses; and structure and toxicity profiles of new drugs that mimic existing drugs determined hazardous by the above criteria. There are 157 drugs identified on the NIOSH Drug Alert list that NIOSH recommends handling as hazardous materials to avoid occupational exposure. These include chemotherapy drugs, hormones (e.g., estrogens), and antibiotics.

In comments to EPA on EPA's August 2010 guidance document, *Best Management Practices for Unused Pharmaceuticals at Health Care Facilities*, the state of Minnesota noted that because EPA has not reviewed any pharmaceuticals for regulation as hazardous waste since the promulgation of RCRA regulations (i.e., 1980), some dangerous pharmaceuticals are not subject to more rigorous regulation as hazardous or acute hazardous waste. Specifically, the state said:

> The proliferation of pharmaceutical development since the promulgation of RCRA regulations, coupled with the absence of any updates to the U- or P-lists, results in some extremely dangerous pharmaceutical waste (e.g., chemotherapeutic drugs) not being listed or characteristic once fully evaluated, while other pharmaceutical waste (e.g., warfarin and nicotine) that is much less hazardous in finished drug form is regulated as acutely toxic waste. The fact that there is still no federal mandatory waste management regulation for most chemotherapy drugs is alarming. Encouraging health care facilities to manage NIOSH hazardous drugs as hazardous waste does not adequately address the danger.

In addition, in its comments on EPA's 2008 UWR amendment, the state of Minnesota also reflects the problem with not having a regular process to evaluate pharmaceuticals for hazardous waste regulation. Specifically, the state said:

> The P-List of hazardous waste is out-of-date to the extent that it is largely irrelevant with regard to currently used pharmaceuticals

---

[8] This potentially defines possible candidate U-list pharmaceuticals. U-listing requires additional justification beyond an LD50 value.

and hence currently generated pharmaceutical waste. Many of the hazardous pharmaceuticals that are listed on either the P-List or U-List are no longer in common use. At the same time, a plethora of new, more toxic pharmaceuticals are not listed at all, despite the fact that they are being generated in a wide variety of health care facilities.

Health Care Facilities May be Unaware of Their RCRA Obligations

EPA has learned, from its communication with stakeholders, and stated in its cost-benefit analysis of the 2008 Universal Waste proposed rule, that "many healthcare facilities have been unable to comply with the RCRA hazardous waste regulations as they relate to hazardous pharmaceutical wastes and often manage these wastes improperly."[9] According to EPA, health care workers, retail pharmacy employees, and other pharmaceutical generators are often unfamiliar with or confused by RCRA hazardous waste management requirements, prompting them to improperly dispose of hazardous pharmaceuticals as municipal or bulk wastes. Outreach and enforcement efforts undertaken in Minnesota and Washington have indicated that confusion and a lack of awareness exist among health care facilities, such as hospitals, regarding the applicability of RCRA regulations to their pharmaceutical wastes. EPA also acknowledges that many health care-related facilities are unaware of their RCRA obligations, or, even if there is knowledge of RCRA, they have problems training workers to properly manage hazardous wastes. ORCR staff informed us that they could implement outreach activities to assist with education and compliance. However, at this time, EPA does not have a comprehensive outreach and compliance assistance plan for HWPs that states can use to improve RCRA compliance.

Improper Management of Pharmaceuticals in Health Care Facilities

State environmental agencies in Minnesota and Washington have conducted outreach and enforcement activities in response to confusion and unfamiliarity among the health care industry about RCRA rules for HWPs. For example, the Minnesota Pollution Control Agency developed a Health Care Initiative in 2002 to address widespread noncompliance with RCRA regulations. They began with an outreach program that provided training to the health care industry, followed by inspections and enforcement. From 2004 to 2007, they identified 2 million pounds of pharmaceuticals that had been properly managed as a result of compliance and enforcement activities. The Washington Department of Ecology created enforcement guidance and conducted outreach activities to educate hospitals about proper disposal of pharmaceutical wastes. These outreach efforts were in response to hospitals' requests for clarification on how to identify and manage HWPs, particularly controlled substances.

---

[9] Assessment of the Potential Costs, Benefits, and Other Impacts of Adding Pharmaceuticals to the Universal Waste Rule, as Proposed. EPA-HQ-RCRA-2007-0932-0010, October 2008, page 1.

In addition, EPA Regions 1 and 2 have increased enforcement activities related to improper disposal of hazardous pharmaceuticals. In 2004, Region 1 notified 250 hospitals in New England of its intention to enforce hazardous waste laws for health care facilities. In 2003 and 2004, Region 2 identified violations at health care facilities, leading to fines ranging from $40,000 to $280,000. In 2010, five hospitals and nursing homes were cited by the New York Attorney General for failure to properly identify, track, and dispose of pharmaceuticals and other wastes defined as hazardous waste under RCRA.

EPA Is Developing a New Pharmaceutical Rulemaking

In 2008, EPA proposed an amendment to its 1995 UWR to provide a system for disposing HWPs that is protective of public health and the environment. The proposed rule was aimed at streamlining the current regulations governing HWPs to ensure that larger quantities of these wastes are managed properly. By March 2009, EPA staff stated they had received approximately 100 stakeholder comments on the rule. Stakeholders commenting on the proposal expressed concerns over the lack of notification and tracking requirements for facilities that handle and transport universal pharmaceutical wastes. According to EPA, generators of HWPs also have expressed concerns related to making hazardous waste determinations, changes in generator status resulting from generation of acutely hazardous waste, regulation of additional pharmaceuticals as RCRA hazardous waste, and accumulation time limits.

Shortly after receiving and reviewing public comments in 2009, EPA determined that the 2008 UW proposal could not be used as a basis for a final rule that would address commenters' concerns. In the response to the draft report (see Appendix B) ORCR staff said that in the fall of 2010, they began developing a new proposal for the health care industry for managing hazardous waste pharmaceuticals. ORCR staff further stated that in September of 2011 the Agency completed Early Guidance, the first of three major milestones in its rule development process, and completed Option Selection, the second milestone, in April of 2012. They acknowledged that there are issues not properly addressed within the current version of the proposed rule and are working to identify areas that need to be addressed in the future version of the rule. Until a rule is finalized, concerns raised by pharmaceutical waste generators related to identification and management of hazardous pharmaceuticals, generator status, and accumulation time limits remain unresolved. EPA has recently stated on its UWR website that "the Agency has decided to develop another proposal for health care facility-specific regulations for the management of hazardous pharmaceutical wastes in order to provide a regulatory scheme that addresses the unique issues that hospitals, pharmacies and other health care-related facilities face. It is anticipated that the proposal will be available for public comment in Spring 2013." EPA has also included updated information on the UWR status in the EPA Fall 2011 Regulatory Agenda.

Conclusion

For more than 30 years, EPA has not used its RCRA authority to determine whether pharmaceuticals may qualify as hazardous waste. This may mean some drugs are disposed and managed in ways that are not safe for humans and the environment. EPA's belief that there is widespread noncompliance in the health care industry with RCRA hazardous waste regulations further compounds the potential risks to human health and the environment from unregulated HWPs. In addition, the idle status of EPA's rule to improve management of HWPs, coupled with its primary reliance on "best management practices" to ensure human health and environmental protection, represent small steps in an environment where hundreds of pharmaceutical products are widely used throughout the nation. EPA has recently published its intent to develop another proposal to address the management of pharmaceutical wastes at health care facilities. Over 100 drugs have been identified by other federal agencies as hazardous pharmaceuticals, whereas EPA has identified 31 hazardous pharmaceutical compounds. If EPA's hazardous waste rules do not keep up with new drug development or ensure that regulated entities understand and comply with their obligations, uncertainties about human health and environmental risks from hazardous pharmaceuticals are likely to grow.

Recommendations

We recommend the Assistant Administrator for Solid Waste and Emergency Response:

1. Identify and review existing pharmaceuticals to determine whether they qualify for regulation as hazardous waste.

2. Establish a process to review new pharmaceuticals to determine whether they qualify for regulation as hazardous waste.

3. Develop a nationally consistent outreach and compliance assistance plan to help states address challenges that health care facilities, and others as needed, have in complying with RCRA regulations for managing HWPs.

Agency Response and OIG Evaluation

We reviewed the Office of Solid Waste and Emergency Response's (OSWER's) comments and made changes to the report as appropriate. Appendix B provides the full text of OSWER's response and the OIG's comments.

OSWER does not clearly agree or disagree with recommendations 1 and 2, and agrees with recommendation 3. In its response to recommendation 1, OSWER agrees that pharmaceuticals are a category of chemicals that need attention and stated that it has recently completed a research effort to identify and evaluate new and existing pharmaceuticals for potential addition to the lists of regulated hazardous wastes. In its response to recommendation 2, OSWER states that it will consider the next steps it can take when it completes actions on recommendation 1. OSWER acknowledges that the next steps could include activities consistent with OIG recommendation 2. We will continue to recommend that EPA adopt a process to review new pharmaceuticals to determine whether they qualify for regulation as hazardous waste, because listing of hazardous waste is integral to the RCRA program.

All recommendations are listed as unresolved. In its 90-day response to this report, EPA should indicate agreement or disagreement with recommendations 1 and 2 and include a detailed corrective action plan with estimated milestone dates for all recommendations.

Status of Recommendations and Potential Monetary Benefits

	RECOMMENDATIONS					POTENTIAL MONETARY BENEFITS (in $000s)	
Rec. No.	Page No.	Subject	Status[1]	Action Official	Planned Completion Date	Claimed Amount	Agreed-To Amount
1	11	Identify and review existing pharmaceuticals to determine whether they qualify for regulation as hazardous waste.	U	Assistant Administrator for Solid Waste and Emergency Response			
2	11	Establish a process to review new pharmaceuticals to determine whether they qualify for regulation as hazardous waste.	U	Assistant Administrator for Solid Waste and Emergency Response			
3	11	Develop a nationally consistent outreach and compliance assistance plan to help states address challenges that health care facilities, and others as needed, have in complying with RCRA regulations for managing HWPs.	U	Assistant Administrator for Solid Waste and Emergency Response			

[1] O = recommendation is open with agreed-to corrective actions pending
C = recommendation is closed with all agreed-to actions completed
U = recommendation is unresolved with resolution efforts in progress

Pharmaceuticals Meeting
Acute Hazardous Waste Criteria

Pharmaceutical	P/U code	Rat Oral LD50 (mg/kg)
NIOSH-listed hazardous pharmaceuticals not listed as EPA hazardous waste		
Carmustine	None	20
Cisplatin	None	25.8
Colchicine	None	26
Dactinomycin	None	7.2
Mechlorethamine	None	10
Oxytocin	None	20.52
Thiotepa	None	23
Vinorelbine tartrate	None	26
P-listed RCRA hazardous waste pharmaceuticals		
Arsenic trioxide	P012	14.6
Epinephrine	P042	30
Nicotine	P075	50
Nitroglycerin	P081	105
Phentermine	P046	Rat oral LD50 not found
Physostigmine	P204	4.5
Physostigmine salicylate	P188	Rat oral LD50 Not found
Warfarin >0.3%	P001	1.6
U-listed RCRA hazardous waste pharmaceuticals with P-level LD50 values		
Melphalan	U150	11.2
Mitomycin C	U010	30
Uracil mustard	U237	3.55

Source: OIG analysis. Rat oral LD50 values were obtained from toxicity data at the National Library of Medicine ChemIDPlus Advanced website. The value for Vinorelbine tartrate was obtained from an Internet Material Safety Data Sheet, and Colchicine was obtained from a Food and Drug Administration abstract. The NIOSH chemicals listed are those we could identify that meet EPA's criteria for regulation as acute hazardous waste but are not regulated.

Agency Response to Draft Report and OIG Comment

MEMORANDUM

SUBJECT: Response to the Office of Inspector General Draft Audit Report, *EPA Inaction in Identifying Hazardous Pharmaceutical Waste May Result in Unsafe Disposal*

FROM: Mathy Stanislaus
Assistant Administrator

TO: Elizabeth Grossman
Acting Assistant Inspector General for Program Evaluation
Office of Inspector General

Thank you for the opportunity to review and respond to the Office of Inspector General (OIG) draft audit report, *EPA Inaction in Identifying Hazardous Pharmaceutical Waste May Result in Unsafe Disposal*. The purpose of this memorandum is to transmit the Office of Solid Waste and Emergency Response's (OSWER) response to the OIG draft report and its recommendations. This memorandum addresses the report's recommendations; Attachment 1 provides detailed comments on the report.

Before responding to the recommendations, however, I would like to provide some background on the Resource Conservation and Recovery Act (RCRA) hazardous waste identification regulations. This serves as context for the issue that you have raised on pharmaceuticals. The basic RCRA waste identification regulations were first established in 1980. Major revisions were made in response to the Hazardous and Solid Waste Amendments (HSWA) of 1984. We added additional listings of hazardous wastes required under HSWA for wastes from specific sources; the final listing was completed in 2005. In 1990 we revised the Toxicity Characteristic, also in response to a HSWA directive. Since that time, new technologies, such as nanotechnology and biotechnology, and new and modified organic and inorganic chemicals are constantly being developed, generating new wastes that may pose risks when disposed of. Resources to evaluate new waste streams and regulate them appropriately are increasingly limited. Within these limitations, however, we are working to address those that most need attention.

OIG RECOMMENDATIONS AND OSWER RESPONSES

OIG Recommendation 1: Identify and review existing pharmaceuticals to determine whether they qualify for regulation as hazardous waste.

OSWER Response 1:

OSWER agrees that pharmaceuticals are a category of chemicals that need attention and has recently completed a research effort to identify and evaluate new and existing pharmaceuticals for potential addition to the lists of regulated hazardous wastes.

To make the best use of our very limited resources, we have prioritized our work in a number of ways. First, we focused on pharmaceuticals that had been identified as chemicals of concern in processes designed to identify pharmaceuticals of high risk already conducted by other federal agencies. We used lists developed by the National Institute for Occupational Safety and Health (NIOSH) and the Occupational Safety and Health Administration (OSHA).[10] Second, we gathered readily available existing toxicological information about these pharmaceuticals. Third, we compared the existing available information to the defined regulatory standard for identifying acutely hazardous waste. The work that we conducted and the results we found were similar to the research recently done by your staff as part of your investigation and presented in the Appendix to your report.

OSWER is now reviewing the results of this project and deciding on next steps that could be completed within available resources to address identified potential risks from disposal of pharmaceuticals. (See Attachment for further discussion regarding the listing of hazardous waste pharmaceuticals.) Possible next steps range from taking no action to potential regulatory considerations. We caution that, due to limited resources, the work we have conducted is narrow in scope and has a number of limitations. As we evaluate next steps, we will consider whether and how these limitations could be addressed with available resources.

OIG Response: OSWER does not clearly agree or disagree with this recommendation. However, OSWER agrees that pharmaceuticals are a category of chemicals that need attention and stated that it has recently completed a research effort to identify and evaluate new and existing pharmaceuticals for potential addition to the lists of regulated hazardous wastes. In its 90-day response to the final report, OSWER should agree or disagree with the recommendation, and, as appropriate, provide actual or estimated milestone completion dates for actions to respond to this recommendation. In addition OSWER should provide a complete description of its corrective action plan for this recommendation. This recommendation will be designated as unresolved in the final report.

OIG Recommendation 2: Establish a process to review new pharmaceuticals to determine whether they qualify for regulation as hazardous waste.

---

[10] *NIOSH List of Antineoplastic and Other Hazardous Drugs in Healthcare Settings 2010* (157 drugs) and OSHA Technical Manual, Section VI, Chapter 2, Appendix VI:2-1 Some Common Drugs Considered Hazardous (61 drugs).

OSWER Response 2:

  As part of OSWER's decision on next steps as discussed in Response 1, we will consider the appropriate next steps to take given significant resource constraints and competing priorities. The next steps to be considered could include a process to review newly developed pharmaceuticals.

OIG Response: OSWER's response to recommendation 2 is linked to its response on recommendation 1, which OSWER does not clearly agree or disagree with. OSWER states that it will consider the next steps it can take when it completes actions on recommendation 1. OSWER acknowledges that the next steps could include activities consistent with OIG recommendation 2. We continue to recommend that EPA adopt a process to review new pharmaceuticals to determine whether they qualify for regulation as hazardous waste, because listing of hazardous waste is integral to the RCRA program. As stated in EPA's *RCRA Orientation Manual*, "Proper hazardous waste identification is essential to the success of the RCRA program." This recommendation will be designated as unresolved in the final report. In its 90-day response to the report, EPA should indicate agreement or disagreement with recommendation 2, and, as appropriate, provide estimated milestone completion dates for agreed-to corrective actions along with a description of the corrective action plan.

OIG Recommendation 3: Develop a nationally consistent outreach and compliance assistance plan to help states address challenges health care facilities, and others as needed, have in complying with RCRA regulations for managing HPWs.[11]

OSWER Response 3:

  OSWER agrees with the recommendation. Our response includes three planned phases: 1) continue ongoing outreach and compliance assistance for the current regulations; 2) propose revisions to RCRA regulations to more effectively address hazardous waste pharmaceuticals in the health care sector; and 3) as we do for all new rules, develop a communications plan detailing outreach efforts to implement the new regulations.

- Phase 1: We note that OSWER and the Office of Enforcement and Compliance Assurance (OECA) have already done a great deal of work to assist states and the regulated community with implementation of and compliance with the current RCRA regulations for hazardous waste pharmaceuticals. Examples are listed below. Within available resources, we will continue these kinds of outreach and compliance assistance efforts for the current regulations.

    1. Healthcare Environmental Resource Center (HERC) - HERC provides compliance assistance and pollution prevention information to the healthcare sector. It is funded by OECA's Office of Compliance, managed by the Office of Chemical Safety and Pollution Prevention, and OSWER provides technical expertise on RCRA. HERC offers compliance assistance to healthcare facilities

---

[11] Hazardous pharmaceutical waste.

and veterinarians, and a center devoted to dentists is currently being developed. (http://www.hercenter.org)

2. "Managing Pharmaceutical Waste: A 10-Step Blueprint for Healthcare Facilities in the United States" (The Blueprint) - The Blueprint provides hospitals a step-by-step guide for developing and implementing a comprehensive pharmaceutical waste management program. While the most recent version (revised August 2008) was funded by HERC, the original Blueprint (April 2006) was funded by OSWER and managed by EPA Region 1. The Office of Resource Conservation and Recovery Staff (ORCR) staff reviewed and provided comments on both versions. (http://practicegreenhealth.org/sites/default/files/upload-files/pharmwasteblueprint.pdf)

3. Development of healthcare-specific memoranda: Through guidance memoranda, OSWER has addressed various healthcare-specific pharmaceutical waste issues that have been raised by the regulated community. For example, most recently, in November 2011,ORCR issued guidance for managing containers that held P-listed pharmaceuticals, most commonly warfarin and nicotine. The guidance outlined several approaches generators may be able to use to address this issue. In particular, the EPA pointed out that only the weight of the residue in the container counts towards the generator status and that the container itself is not a hazardous waste. This guidance has been very well received by the industry.

4. Outreach: OSWER maintains close communication with stakeholders on these issues and has made numerous presentations on pharmaceutical waste issues, including updates on the pharmaceutical rulemaking, at conferences and webinars hosted by the regulated community and by EPA.

- Phase 2: As noted in your report, we are in the process of developing major revisions to the hazardous waste regulations to make them more effective for the health care sector and the hazardous waste pharmaceuticals they generate. This step will help states with implementation and the regulated community with compliance with the RCRA regulations for hazardous waste pharmaceuticals. Our current plans anticipate publication of a proposed rule in March 2013.

- Phase 3: As we do for all new rules, as we complete the revisions to the regulations, OSWER will develop a communications plan detailing outreach steps to assist states with adoption and implementation of the new regulations and to assist the regulated community with learning about and coming into compliance with the new regulations.

OIG Response: OSWER agrees with recommendation 3. OSWER is taking steps to communicate with health care facilities to assist compliance with RCRA regulations for managing HWPs. The activities described meet the intent of the recommendation. However, because estimated or actual milestone dates were not included, this recommendation will be listed as unresolved in the final report. In its 90-day response to the report, EPA should provide estimated or actual completion dates for the milestones.

OSWER welcomes the opportunity to continue working with OIG to implement these recommendations and to strengthen its hazardous waste identification program. If you have any questions, please contact Suzanne Rudzinski, in the Office of Resource Conservation and Recovery, at (703) 308-8895.

Attachment

ATTACHMENT
EPA Comments on OIG February 29, 2012 Draft Report *EPA Inaction in Identifying*
Hazardous Pharmaceutical Waste May Result in Unsafe Disposal

GENERAL COMMENT REGARDING HAZARDOUS WASTE IDENTIFICATION

The report does not appear to fully appreciate the complexities of listing a chemical as a commercial chemical product. The report says (page 3):

> P and U lists of chemicals – hazardous wastes including specific unused chemicals. Chemicals are included on the U list based on toxicity and characteristics. Chemicals are included on the P list if they are acutely toxic. P list chemicals are managed more stringently than U list chemicals.

The report correctly cites the criteria for listing chemicals as P-listed waste. However, the description for U-listed chemicals is much too simplified and does not fully delineate the process for listing a chemical on the U-list. The report states (pages 3 and 7 - 8):

> Pharmaceuticals can be included on the U list if they exhibit any of the hazardous characteristics described above, or if they contain a toxic constituent and are capable of posing a "substantial present or potential hazard to human health or the environment when improperly treated, stored, transported, or disposed of, or otherwise managed."

> Further, we identified at least 21 additional pharmaceuticals with LD50 values between 50 and 500 mg/kg, which are within the range of values found for existing U-list pharmaceuticals.[8]

> [8] This potentially defines possible candidate U-list pharmaceuticals. U-listing requires additional justification beyond an LD50 value.

In fact, the process for listing chemicals on the U-list is not a matter of simply comparing LD50 values. Therefore, the results provided in the report using such a comparison are not meaningful. As the report itself noted (page 3), unless a pharmaceutical exhibits any of the hazardous characteristics, listing a chemical on the U-list requires that the Agency demonstrate that the chemical poses a "substantial present or potential hazard to human health or the environment" when improperly managed. The regulations for this listing approach are set out in 40 CFR 261.11(a)(3). These regulations specify a number of factors that must be considered, including:

- the toxicity and concentrations of the hazardous constituents in the waste,
- the quantity of the waste generated,
- the potential for the constituents to migrate, persist, and bioaccumulate in the environment,
- any cases of environmental damage from improper management, and
- plausible types of management of the waste.

For all recent listings, EPA has used risk assessment tools to assess potential risks from waste management to encompass most of these factors. Furthermore, whether a waste is listed or not depends to a great degree on how the waste is being managed. That is, the waste must present a "substantial" hazard based on "plausible" management practices. Therefore, while the inherent toxicity of a chemical in a waste is important, the other factors in 261.11(a)(3) must be considered in evaluating a chemical for listing as a U-list hazardous waste. This type of assessment requires a large amount of information about a waste, and listing a waste using these criteria requires a significant effort and resources.

OIG Response: The OIG acknowledges the potential complexity beyond LD50 values for U-listed waste. The report specifically states criteria for U-listing in *EPA Definition of Hazardous Waste* Chapter 1 pages 2-3, and also states in Chapter 2 footnote 8 page 8 that U-listing requires additional justification.

SPECIFIC COMMENTS

Entire report:

1. When referring to wastes that are currently identified by RCRA regulation as hazardous waste, recommend using the term "Hazardous Waste Pharmaceutical" (HWP) instead of "Hazardous Pharmaceutical Waste" (HPW). Because "hazardous waste" is a specific regulatory phrase, it is clearer to use it directly in the term. Also recommend using another term, such as "non-regulated pharmaceutical waste" for discarded pharmaceuticals that may be of concern, but are not currently regulated under RCRA. This would clarify whether the text is referring to RCRA-regulated or non-regulated pharmaceutical wastes.

OIG Response: The term "Hazardous Pharmaceutical Waste (HPW)" has been changed in the report to "Hazardous Waste Pharmaceutical (HWP)" as requested by OSWER. We note that this represents a recent change, as HPW was used in prior EPA publications such as the 2008 proposed universal waste rule and the 2010 draft *Guidance Document: Best Management Practices for Unused Pharmaceuticals at Health Care Facilities*. HWP was most recently used in OSWER's *Management Standards for Hazardous Waste Pharmaceuticals* published in the Fall 2011 Regulatory Agenda. However, we note that OSWER continues to use the term "hazardous pharmaceutical wastes" in recent updates to its UWR website. We suggest that OSWER consistently use "hazardous waste pharmaceuticals" in all future publications. The report uses "unregulated HWP" to refer to pharmaceutical wastes not currently regulated by RCRA, instead of "non-regulated pharmaceutical waste."

2. Recommend using the term "active pharmaceutical ingredients (APIs)" when discussing chemicals in the environment since environmental analysis tests for individual APIs.

OIG Response: This change will not be incorporated, as it would add unneeded complexity to the terminology of the report.

3. Background, left-hand column, 2nd sentence: Add drinking water to the list of types of water where APIs are found.

OIG Response: "Drinking water" added as suggested.

4. Background, left-hand column: When discussing APIs in water it is important to note that: 1) While improper disposal of drugs contributes to the presence of APIs in our nation's waters, other contributions include excretion and pass-through from POTWs; and 2) Available studies identify very few APIs in water that are regulated hazardous wastes.

OIG Response: This point will not be added to the Background in the At a Glance section. The additional level of detail is not appropriate for this section, which is intended to provide a snapshot of what the report is about.

5. "What We Found," 1st paragraph, 5th sentence: For accuracy, revise to read "We identified eight chemicals found in pharmaceuticals that meet EPA's criteria for regulation as acute hazardous waste but wastes containing these chemicals are not regulated, unless they exhibit a characteristic."

OIG Response: The important point in this statement is that these pharmaceuticals have not been specifically identified by EPA for regulation as acute hazardous waste even though they meet the toxicity criteria. "As such" added to the end of the sentence for clarification.

6. "What We Found," 1st paragraph, 6th sentence: For accuracy, revise to read "There are over 100 drugs that federal occupational safety organizations have identified as hazardous but have only recently been reviewed by EPA to determine whether they may qualify as hazardous waste. As a result of comments received on the proposed rule for pharmaceutical wastes, EPA started an examination of the lists from OSHA and NIOSH for potential candidates for listing as commercial chemical products. EPA found that relatively few of them would meet the criteria for listing as acute hazardous waste under the commercial chemical product listings (40 CFR 261.33(e)), similar results to those found by the OIG in its work for this study."

OIG Response: No change was made because the referenced sentence is accurate as written. A new sentence was added to acknowledge EPA's stated efforts: "EPA staff stated they have started examining these drugs for listing as hazardous waste."

7. "What We Found," 2nd paragraph, 3rd sentence: Delete and replace with "This may result in mismanagement of hazardous waste pharmaceuticals." Note: RCRA regulations generally allow drain disposal of HW. The domestic sewage exclusion of 40 CFR 261.4(a)(1)(ii) is designed to avoid duplicative regulation under the Clean Water Act and RCRA and thus defers coverage of domestic sewage to the Clean Water Act regulations.

OIG Response: Sentence changed as suggested.

8. "What We Found," 3rd paragraph: Delete 2nd sentence.

OIG Response: No change was made. The sentence states that no action has occurred on the 2008 UWR since 2009. EPA states in the Fall 2011 Regulatory Agenda, "…EPA is considering re-proposing healthcare facility-specific regulations for the management of hazardous pharmaceutical wastes…," but no specific action has yet been taken.

9. "What We Found," 3rd paragraph, 3rd sentence: For accuracy, revise to read "EPA staff informed us that, due to substantial negative public comments received on the 2008 universal waste proposal, the Agency is developing a revised proposal for regulation of hazardous waste pharmaceuticals at healthcare facilities."

OIG Response: Sentence modified to incorporate this comment.

Table of Contents:

10. Suggest including the word "findings" in the title of Chapter 2 for clarity.

OIG Response: No change was made. This is an editorial comment and it is our opinion that the title is an appropriate description of the contents of the chapter.

Chapter 1:

11. Page 1, Background, 2nd sentence: Add a clarifying footnote at the end of the sentence to read "Note: very few, if any antibiotics and endocrine disrupters are HWP. In addition, they do not meet the current hazardous waste listing/characteristic criteria."

OIG Response: No change was made. This statement in the report is an accurate summary of statements in the GAO report, *Environmental Health: Action Needed to Sustain Agencies' Collaboration on Pharmaceuticals in Drinking Water*, August 2011. Further, EPA provides no evidence for the statement that "few, if any antibiotics and endocrine disrupters are HWP."

12. Page 1, Background, 3rd and 4th sentences: Recommend providing references to sources for information presented about detrimental effects of pharmaceuticals on aquatic species, etc.

OIG Response: These statements are based on information in the EPA *Health Services Industry Study Management and Disposal of Unused Pharmaceuticals (Interim Technical Report)* August 2008; and the GAO report, *Action Needed to Sustain Agencies' Collaboration on Pharmaceuticals in Drinking Water*, August 2011.

13. Page 1, Background, 2nd paragraph, 1st sentence: Replace definition of pharmaceutical, or explain the source of this definition. At this time, EPA does not have a formal definition of pharmaceutical. EPA proposed a regulatory definition of pharmaceutical in the 2008 proposal, but since the rule

was not finalized, that definition is not in place. FDA may have a definition that would serve the purpose.

OIG Response: This definition is from the 2008 proposal. "In the 2008 proposed universal waste rule," added for clarity.

14. Page 1-2, Background, last sentence: For clarity, revise to read "A Pharmaceutical becomes a waste when a decision is made to dispose of it. This can include unused but expired drugs (e.g., personal medications) and waste materials containing excess drugs, such as syringes, IV bags, tubing, vials, etc."

OIG Response: No change was made. Footnote 1 specifies that EPA does not regulate pharmaceuticals until they are discarded as waste, which is when a decision is made to dispose of them.

15. Page 1, Footnote 1: Revise to read "Under RCRA, EPA can not regulate pharmaceuticals until a decision is made to dispose of it."

OIG Response: No change was made. Footnote 1 specifies that EPA does not regulate pharmaceuticals until they are discarded as waste, which is when a decision is made to dispose of them.

16. Page 2, Footnote 2: To incorporate information provided by public commenters on the 2008 proposed rule, revise to read "Reverse distributors are private companies that provide a service to the health care industry by determining credit eligibility on returned pharmaceuticals and by facilitating the receipt of proper credit."

OIG Response: The definition of distributors was taken directly from the 2010 EPA draft *Guidance Document: Best Management Practices for Unused Pharmaceuticals at Health Care Facilities.*

17. Page 2, Background, Last sentence: For accuracy, revise to read "The domestic sewage exclusion at 40 CFR 261.4(a)(1)(ii) generally allows facilities to flush pharmaceuticals down the drain. However, due to the detection of active pharmaceutical ingredients in the environment, EPA recommends that facilities not dispose of their pharmaceuticals down the drain."

OIG Response: The sentence is accurate as written, and was used by EPA in its 2010 draft *Guidance Document: Best Management Practices for Unused Pharmaceuticals at Health Care Facilities.* At the beginning of the sentence, we added the words "Although the domestic sewage exclusion generally allows facilities to flush pharmaceuticals down the drain," to address this comment.

18. Page 2, EPA Definition of Hazardous Waste, 3rd and 4th sentences: For accuracy, revise to read "Federally, any facility, such as a hospital or other health facility, that generates more than 100 kg

(220 lbs.) and less than 1000 kg (2200 lbs) of hazardous waste per month, is a small quantity generator (SQG) under RCRA. A facility that generates greater than 1 kg (2.2 lbs.) of acute hazardous waste per month and/or 1000 kg (2200 lbs.) or more of hazardous waste per month is a large quantity generator (LQG) under RCRA. Facilities that generate less than SQGs and LQGs per month have minimal RCRA requirements. Both SQGs and LQGs are subject to full RCRA hazardous waste regulation. Full RCRA regulations generally include management standards for waste accumulation and required transportation by a hazardous waste transporter to a permitted hazardous waste treatment, storage and disposal facility. " DOT regulations require certain container packaging for transport, and RCRA defers to DOT on this.

OIG Response: The sentences are accurate as written, and the suggested revisions provide a level of detail not necessary for this report and, in our opinion, will impede readability of the report.

19. Page 2, "corrosivity": For accuracy, revise to read "wastes that are extremely acidic or alkaline (basic)."

OIG Response: OIG's definition is accurate. It is identical with the definitions in the EPA's *RCRA Orientation Manual 2011*.

20. Page 3, c: For accuracy, revise to read "Chemicals are included on the U-list based on toxicity or other characteristics. Chemicals are included on the P-list if they are acutely toxic. P-list chemicals are regulated when generated in lower quantities than U-list chemicals."

OIG Response: Sentences changed as suggested.

21. Page 3, 1st full sentence: For accuracy, revise to read "P-listed wastes are identified as acute hazardous waste because the waste has been found to be fatal to humans or animals above certain thresholds/doses."

OIG Response: Sentence changed as suggested.

22. Page 3, Footnote 4: For accuracy, revise to read "The LD_{50} and LC_{50} value is a measure of acute toxicity and indicates the ability of a toxic or poisonous substance to kill half the population in animal studies within the study's timeframe."

OIG Response: Footnote wording changed to "The LD50 and LC50 value is a measure of acute toxicity, and indicates the ability of a toxic or poisonous substance to kill half the population in animal studies after a specified test duration."

23. Page 3, EPA Definition of Hazardous Waste, last paragraph, first sentence: For clarity, revise to read "Pharmaceuticals can be included on the U-list if they exhibit any of the four hazardous characteristics…"

OIG Response: "Four" added to the sentence as suggested.

24. Page 3, Volume of Hazardous Pharmaceutical Waste, 3rd and 4th sentences: For accuracy, revise to read "However, estimates of the volume of HWP may be understated because under federal regulations, only large quantity generators are required to report their hazardous waste types and volumes."

OIG Response: A new sentence was added after the fourth sentence: "Further, federal regulations require only large quantity generators to report their hazardous waste types and volumes to EPA."

25. Page 3, Footnote 5: For clarity, revise to read "Hazardous waste generators producing more than 2,200 pounds of hazardous waste, or more than 2.2 pounds of acute hazardous waste, in a calendar month must report the waste type and volume to EPA every 2 years."

OIG Response: Sentence changed as suggested.

26. Page 3-4, sentence beginning "EPA estimates…": Recommend additional context such as how much total hazardous waste is generated per year.

OIG Response: We added to footnote 5: "The total volume of hazardous waste reported in 2009 was approximately 35 million tons."

27. Page 4, EPA's Best Management Practices Guidance for Pharmaceuticals, last sentence: For accuracy revise to read "The draft guidance describes BMPs that EPA recommends to health care facilities, long-term care facilities, medical clinics, and doctors' offices, when managing and disposing of unused pharmaceuticals. Numerous comments were received on the draft BMPs."

OIG Response: No change was made. The statement is accurate as written and adding the suggested additional text is not necessary for purposes of the OIG's report.

28. Page 4, last 2 sentences: For accuracy, revise to read: "In 2009, EPA summarized comments on the proposed rule. There was substantial negative comment on the proposed rule such that the Agency decided that it could not address the comments without re-proposing a new rule. Since the fall of 2010, the Agency has been actively developing a new proposed rule that addresses the comments received on the Universal Waste proposal."

OIG Response: We added the following new sentences to reflect EPA's current position on the rulemaking: "According to EPA, there was substantial negative comment on the proposed rule such that the Agency decided that it could not address the comments without re-proposing a new rule. EPA has recently stated that the Agency has decided to develop another proposal for healthcare facility-specific regulations for the management of hazardous waste pharmaceuticals."

29. Page 5, Other Federal Agency Hazardous Drug Lists, 2nd to last sentence: For accuracy, revise to read: "OSHA developed a hazardous drug list in the early 1990s and it remains a primary

reference for health care facilities for identifying drugs that may pose occupational risks to employees."

OIG Response: No was made change. The statement is accurate as written.

Chapter 2:

30. Page 7, 1ˢᵗ sentence: For accuracy, revise to read "Although EPA has the authority under RCRA, it has not added to its regulations pharmaceuticals that may qualify as hazardous waste since 1980."

OIG Response: Sentence changed as suggested.

31. Page 7, 5ᵗʰ sentence: For accuracy, revise to read "However, the rule was stalled during the last half of 2009 and in early 2010. In the fall of 2010, EPA decided it would need to revise the proposed UWR or create a new rule. "

OIG Response: To reflect EPA's current position, we changed the sentence from "However, the rule has been stalled since 2009 and EPA just recently decided it would determine the need to revise the proposed UWR or create a new rule," to "However, the rule has been stalled since 2009 and EPA just recently decided it would develop another proposal for healthcare facility-specific regulations for the management of HWPs."

32. Page 7, 6ᵗʰ sentence: For accuracy, revise to read "Given the proliferation of pharmaceutical development since RCRA was enacted, EPA inaction on adding to its regulations pharmaceuticals that qualify as hazardous waste may result in unsafe disposal and releases of dangerous pharmaceuticals into the environment."

OIG Response: Sentence revised as suggested.

33. Page 7-8, end of 1ˢᵗ incomplete paragraph: Revise to reflect information in the General Comment on Hazardous Waste Identification.

OIG Response: No change was made. Additional requirements for U-listing are noted in the footnote.

34. Page 8, 1ˢᵗ full paragraph, 2ⁿᵈ sentence: For accuracy, revised to read "Currently, EPA recommends RCRA guidelines as a BMP for managing NIOSH-listed hazardous materials that are not currently regulated as HWP." For completeness, OIG should provide a citation for this statement.

OIG Response: The statement is accurate as written. The source is EPA's 2010 draft *Guidance Document: Best Management Practices for Unused Pharmaceuticals at Health Care Facilities*. However, OIG has added text from the draft Guidance Document to clarify that RCRA does not require facilities to manage NIOSH-listed hazardous materials the same as RCRA hazardous waste.

35. Page 9, 1st full paragraph: Add a reference to the "2008 Universal Waste proposed rule."

OIG Response: Text added to the first sentence on page 9 to clarify that the reference is to the 2008 Universal Waste proposed rule.

36. Page 9, 1st full paragraph, 2nd sentence: Explain, or delete the term "bulk waste."

OIG Response: The term is from the 2008 Universal Waste proposed rule: page 73530, Federal Register Vol. 73, No. 232, December 2, 2008.

37. Page 10, 1st paragraph: It would be helpful to explain what regulatory requirement the New York Attorney General used to cite hospitals for disposing of pharmaceutical wastes down sinks and toilets. NY may have more stringent regulations regarding drain disposal of hazardous wastes than the current federal RCRA program, which includes the domestic sewage exclusion of 40 CFR 261.4(a)(1)(ii).

OIG Response: The statement is based on public information released by the New York Attorney General. The sentence has been modified to address only violations clearly identified as federal RCRA violations.

38. Page 10, Title - EPA Pharmaceutical Waste Rulemaking Has Stalled: The title appears to be a remnant from before the section was updated to include recent rule development activity. Also see next comment for further updates. For accuracy, revise to reflect progress the Agency has made developing a new proposed rule to read "EPA is Making Progress On a New Pharmaceutical Waste Rulemaking."

OIG Response: Title changed to "EPA Is Developing a New Pharmaceutical Rulemaking"

39. Page 10: 3rd paragraph, 1st – 2nd sentences: To update and for accuracy, revise to read "Shortly after receiving and reviewing public comments in 2009, EPA determined that the 2008 UW proposal could not be used as a basis for a final rule that would address commenters' concerns. ORCR staff said that in the fall of 2010, they began developing a new proposal for the health care industry for managing hazardous waste pharmaceuticals. In September of 2011 the Agency completed Early Guidance, the first of three major milestones in its rule development process, and expects to complete Option Selection, the second milestone, in April of 2012."

OIG Response: Sentences added as suggested, changed to reflect Agency completion of Option Selection.

40. Page 11, 2nd sentence: For accuracy, revise to read "EPA's belief that there is widespread noncompliance in the health care industry with RCRA hazardous waste regulations suggests that there may be potential risks to human health and the environment from regulated hazardous waste pharmaceuticals."

OIG Response: No change was made. This is an editorial comment that is not materially different than OIG's original conclusions.

41. Page 11, 3rd – 5th sentences: For accuracy, revise to read "In addition, because EPA's rule to improve management of HWP must be re-proposed, the current RCRA HW generator regulations continue apply to generators of HWPs. The RCRA HW generator regulations can be challenging for healthcare facilities, which may result in non-compliance over the short term. Also, over 100 drugs have been identified by other federal agencies as pharmaceuticals that pose potential hazards, whereas EPA only regulates 31 pharmaceutical compounds as listed hazardous wastes and additional pharmaceutical compounds as characteristic hazardous wastes. The Agency has recently conducted a review of other federal agencies' lists to begin to address this issue." Note: The Agency does not rely on best management practices or BMPs to regulate pharmaceuticals that are hazardous waste, the current RCRA regulations are in effect for hazardous waste pharmaceuticals.

OIG Response: No change was made. These are OIG conclusions.

Appendix A:

42. Page 13, Table, For accuracy, revise to read "P-listed RCRA Hazardous Waste pharmaceuticals."

OIG Response: "Hazardous" added to the heading as suggested.

43. Page 13, Table: For accuracy, for phentermine and physostigmine salicylate, add a footnote indicating the toxicity exposure route and LD dose that was the basis for the P-listing. Without the footnote, the chart seems to indicate that because no rat oral LD50 was found, there was no reason to list the chemical. However, both chemicals were listed based on toxicology information for one of three exposure routes.

OIG Response: No change was made. The statement about the lack of a rat oral LD50 does not imply that there was no reason to list the chemical based on EPA's analysis. It simply states that no rat oral LD50 was found.

44. Page 13, Table: For accuracy, revise column header to read: "U-listed RCRA Hazardous Waste pharmaceuticals with P-level LD50 values."

OIG Response: "Hazardous" added to heading consistent with the suggested change.

Distribution

Office of the Administrator
Assistant Administrator for Solid Waste and Emergency Response
Deputy Assistant Administrator for Solid Waste and Emergency Response
Agency Follow-Up Official (the CFO)
Agency Follow-Up Coordinator
General Counsel
Associate Administrator for Congressional and Intergovernmental Relations
Associate Administrator for External Affairs and Environmental Education
Director, Office of Resource Conservation and Recovery, Office of Solid Waste and
    Emergency Response
Audit Follow-Up Coordinator, Office of Solid Waste and Emergency Response

www.ingramcontent.com/pod-product-compliance
Lightning Source LLC
Chambersburg PA
CBHW081803280526
45789CB00008B/2983